Joy

Poems by Francis Daulerio

Foreword by Maggie Smith

Foreword Copyright © 2021 Maggie Smith
Maggie Smith is the author of five books, including *Good Bones* and the national bestsellers *Keep Moving* and *Goldenrod*. Her work has appeared in the *New York Times, The New Yorker, The Washington Post, The Southern Review,* the *Guardian,* the *Paris Review,* and *The Best American Poetry*. A freelance writer and editor, Smith is on the poetry faculty of Spalding University's MFA program and serves as an Editor at Large for the *Kenyon Review*.

Attention schools and booksellers: Copies are available through Ingram Book Group.

For information contact:
Unsolicited Press
Portland, Oregon
www.unsolicitedpress.com
orders@unsolicitedpress.com

Cover design: Helen Ahpornsiri
Editor: S.R. Stewart

ISBN: 978-1-956692-21-1

for Leah, Genevieve, and Simon

&

for Scott

I'll be the reason your own sap's reviving.
I'll mainline the light to your veins.

—Ali Smith

Contents

II

III

IV

Foreword

It's spring as I write this, and everything is beginning to bloom. The trees are finally bursting into color. Wild violets are purpling the lawns in my neighborhood. It feels like joy made tangible, because here's the thing about joy: it's always here, accessible to us, even when we don't see it.

We say that things "bring us joy," but my experience is that joy is not brought, not really. It's brought *out*. It's like the bulbs sleeping beneath the dirt, like the magnolia blossoms folded tightly in their pods, like the leaves waiting for their time to unfurl.

Fran's work—his writing, his teaching, his caregiving, his being-in-the-world—is bringing out joy. He unearths it, brushes it off, holds it up so we can see what was there all along.

These poems bring out joy in me.
I hope they bring out joy in you, too.

Maggie Smith
April 2021

Joy

Hello!

Good morrow!

Welcome!

Here we are
to greet and grow and live
together in the time lapse of bulbs waking up
through the ground and feeling
their way around the dead
leaves, bits of bark,
spent wicks from New Year's firecrackers
that hid beneath the snow
with frozen holly berries,
and all the other remembrances of winter that,
   if my daughter ever naps,
I will rake with my hands into a wheelbarrow,
schlep across the swollen lawn,
and dump into the compost heap
to rot and feed
next year's children of this year's flowers.

  Do you feel how new we all are?

  How limber?

Like my friend who,

after drinking too much whisky,

climbs out through the downstairs window of my house

so not to disturb those wrens who

built their nest in the Valentine's wreath on our front door,

the one we'll now leave up through June,

until they can properly say goodbye to their children,

downsize to the waterfront

dogwood by my creek,

and reminisce about how the sunlight

broke each morning over the birch in the front yard,

peppering light through its flaky branches

onto the home where their babies learned to fly,

but before that flight turned

their downy brown bodies

into smooth brown specks

coasting further

    and further

       away.

This is supposed to be loud–
a flourish from that half-dead daylily
I bought from a roadside stand,
who pops her head out first
     each year now,
          calling to those still sleeping to
          wake up!
          It is time to billow!
          To stun!
          To flabbergast and awe
          all those sick with winter
          and pale from the interior
          who have forgotten
          how fucking beautiful it is

          to be alive

          right

          now!

Let's get naked,
go down to the river,
baptize our bodies
in the church of fresh dirt, and watch
the tiny hairs on our sun-sick limbs
stand at attention in the cold water
like the empty flagpoles
of undiscovered countries,
basking in the freedom
of knowing no king.

Blossom, friends!

This is the time for it!

All of these budding-out trees are spitting oxygen
for nobody else but you,

you beautiful,

stardusted,

happenstance,

realization of a dream.

Hello.
Good morrow.
Welcome.

One

or

the great big backwards glance

Evening Embryonic

Hallelujah and the falling
rain against the window
all night while we sleep safe
on the inside and lucky—
      nothing but the dark and the hum,
      nothing of the tumult
      outside, no light,
         just floating,
            floating,
         the two of us bedded
         down, and the new
         life further in,
            all three
            quiet and curled,

            heartbeat and rhythm,

            flutter and pump,

               goodnight, goodnight,

                  goodnight.

Good Morning, Blueberry

Awoken early
to the steady rain and a cricket chirp
from the app on my phone
that's tracking fetal growth,
[bigger today
than last week's sweet pea
and the apple seed
the week before]
we live each day marveled
at the unfurling, this
blooming, bit by bit,
today's "blueberry" awakening
some cautious joy within,
and the whole day becomes a showering
of pleasantry and devotion,

> *good morning, love*
> *good morning, wife*
> *good morning, blueberry*
> *hello daybreak,*
> *and fresh start,*
> *and wanting to stay alive*

and everything is hope,
and motion, and runoff,
and thinking in fast forward,
the thaw and the sprouting life,
reminded, too, of that little fruit bush
plopped in the clay
last spring like a premonition,
because we thought we could
make it grow, the burlapped bundle
jam-packed with tiny green
berries that soon faded
near purple,
which the birds quickly plundered,
but how, in the weeks before,
the backyard mornings
were so awake,
Leah laughing from the patio
while I bumbled through
the garden, caked with bliss,
talking the whole time,

> *good morning, blueberry!*
> *kind regards,*
> *cheers to your fresh growth!*

and how bright it was,
before the beaks and the theft
and the learning that no more could grow
without a second,
something about cross pollination,
each plant needing
another to thrive, oh,
how we need each other to thrive—

Blueberry,
I cannot wait to see
what you become,
when you're pushed into this world
that is so full
of anger, and fear, and people
all the time just wanting
to die. Tell me, how could you
do anything but
glimmer?

I'm sorry, but
how can we
do anything
but shine?

On The Bookshelf Is A Little Rock I Took From Walden Pond

We put in the work,
tidy with the details,
elbow grease and all that,
little dishes stacked above
the big ones,
the dryer vent cleared
so the place won't burn,
and all the other
bits of what we learn a life is.

And sure,
the bills don't pay themselves,
my nerves in messy piles
scattered all around the house,
but when the wind's right,
there's lilac through
the window,
and if the panic wakes me up
in the middle of a rough one,
I'll sometimes spot our fox,
the little one with the too-long tail,
muddy footed and screeching

something primal
in the wild,
wild darkness.

Lungs

Nine weeks in,
and this gray-black fuzzy
picture of my daughter
is now breathing,
     sort of.

The ultrasound technician calls it
     practice—
     movement
     to build memory
     so it'll be natural
     on the outside.

Two miles away,
my grandmother's nurse
reminds her how
it works:

     Smell the roses.
     Blow out the candles.

Outside, September's
harvest bolts

in the heat
while the goldenrod topples,
     grown too tall
          for its own
               ambition.

Rutters

Autumn here, again,
and the backyard all aburst
with crimson's quick glow,
the creek, high from last night's
outpour, rushing
leaves down and down and down and
nothing but still
and little crunches
of hooves on oak-drop
as the mating stalk
drags a buck on loop
behind our doe,
she who eats from our hands,
who did not hide like the rest
when we cut our home
into these trees,
and who we love for it
and for her big, glassy eyes,
graybrown coat
now fluffed with coming winter.

But in new November dusk,
everything seems ready for the finish,

especially her suitor, I suppose,
thinking much of himself
for running off the rest,
small as they were
and thinly antlered,
his slow march dragging
muscle and fur and exhaled steam
on this hopeful collision course
with the unwilling,
the awkward quiet of this strange scene
broken only by my wife,
fogging up the window with her breath
and tapping on the pane
yelling, *leave her alone, you prick!*
  Fearing her own pains of labor
  for this child she'd longed for,
  she feels for our girl.
And so how can she not
send me out in defense?
Though under-clothed and, yes, a little drunk,
I can only mimic what I've seen,
lifting my leg slowly, driving it
back against the ground firm,
which I've learned is deer to mean,
  please fuck off, or,
  move along, sir, there'll be none of this here,

to which, and this is true, he stomps back
in reply, this standoff
trade of back and forths continuing
a minute or two until it's clear
enough to him at least
that I'll not be hopping the split rail fence
or wading the creek beyond it
and so pose no threat,
the sexed-up brute leaving me
to his periphery, drifting back
into her orbit, their own small galaxy
spinning off into the forest.

Inside that night, I read
about the government pumping
contraception into suburban wilds,
stifling growth to make room
while we sprawl,
and think maybe she'll be lucky,
a hope we hold for days
until she roams back, alone,
to spend the winter swelling on our scraps,
new life rolling around
inside her.

All Of What We Pass Along & All We Keep Inside

I come from
a long line of people
who have stood
outside
in their underwear
with shotguns
hollering [nervous] obscenities
and [empty] threats
into the darkness.

Shallow Breaths & My Dreaming of Spring

November's early darkness,
and the station wagon full
of stud wood and sheets of
white pine,
my chapped hands cracked across
the steering wheel, winding
toward a bright garage
that I call the woodshop
and my wife calls the garage,
to let the dissonance
of saws and compressed air
drown out my piercing brain,
sick without sunlight,
that old loop of panic
on reel behind my eyes.

Again this year I will build my way out
of this illness,
back to my wife
who knows only splinters
of what I do to myself,
so I can fill back into
my old clothes,

bring the blood back
to my face,
and let all of this
caged light
burst back through
like a solstice,
or that muddy April shine.

Dragging Out The Dead

Tomato plants, browned
by last night's frost,
crumble like pressed flowers
between the pages
of *A Midsummer Night's Dream*,
    blooms cut off
    mid-sentence,
        half open,
                just about to sing.

Love In The Time Of Network News

In my golden years
I hope to find myself more
like the fella in the yellow house around the corner,
the one right on the main road
with the wrought iron bench
out front, all shimmery
with sequined pillows
and Christmas lights all year,
and the little give-one-take-one
wooden library box planted
inches from the shoulder
where the cars burn by on loop
as if to say, *never mind*
the speed of it all,
as if to say
welcome.

Out Past The Light Of The Moon

Sometimes love exists
like autumn—
   birch burning
   in our chests,
      billowing
      bark and sparks.

Sometimes we exist
like a bellows,
   breathing into one another
   so we each may glow
      brighter
         and far
            into our distances.

Tunnels

My daughter kicks
at the red glow
of a penlight
against Leah's bare stomach,
remembering less
with each passing day
and grabbing,
[instinctually]
for a light
no longer within her
reach.

Sweater Weather

You caught me.

I begged for this.

Did the dancing, lit
the candles, beckoned
this blanket
that makes my pop huff and puff
and shove his hands
into his pockets and sit
bitter for five months.

But it's here,
and so on with the whisky
and the cold toes
shoved under
your lover's warm leg
on the sofa by a roarer
for the dark months of watching
out the quiet windows for life,
animals passing in the night,
limbs dropping, weighed with ice.

Everything is here for us.

What better than
to drape into each other,
to love closer,
to warm?

Sartre In My Nursery

Rolling
a second coat of paint
on the walls in my daughter's bedroom,
I hear winter
filling up the creek
beneath our windows.

I hope she learns
how beautiful this all is
long before
the fear
of disappearing
like raindrops
into rivers.

Bloom

There are parts
my wife will always remember:
the exhaustion, hunger,
and the kicking
in her belly.

I'll remember the rain,
and the steam rising
from the streets—
God's last-ditch effort
to tidy things up
a bit before you
got here.

Two

[be here be here be here be here be here
be here be here be here be here be here
be here be here be here be here be here]

Come What May

    I imagine from above
    we must look
    so spastic,
    running blind
    and terrified
    towards some conjured light,
        ever forward,
            and fuck if we'll find
            what for.

The Parts of Space We've Not Yet Seen

God is on the run—
feeling around with his hands
in the darkness
of space, wishing
he'd made just a bit more
light
on Day One.
    It doesn't carry
        like he'd hoped it would.

We're closing in,
so he's packing up
and retreating
like spaghetti western bandits
breaking down camp
and moving deeper
into the mountains,
nothing left behind
but empty cans of beans,
butts of hand-rolled cigarettes,
and embers of a burned out
paradise.

We're more ruthless than he'd figured,
and we're hell-bent
on finding Heaven
on our own terms,
before we're taken
against our will.

    People used to pray,
    used to pick up trash
    outside inner-city schools
    and drop change
    into coffee cups
    for Vietnam vets
    and that used to be enough.

        That's all it took.

But now we're getting restless
and launching rockets
and satellites
and closing in on the new world,
wide-eyed
and dangerous
like Columbus,
and I'll be damned
if God doesn't feel like the *Indian.*

You have to feel sorry for him,
up there looking
over his shoulder,
ducking behind theories
we haven't cracked yet,
hoping he can outlast us.

It's the waiting that has to get to him,
and even God must get scared
up there in all that darkness.

Something We'd Call Heaven

At six weeks old,
my daughter still stares
into lights
like she misses them,
the way I already look
at just slightly younger pictures
of her.

She must still remember
enough to feel
the heat behind her ears,
that tingling of growth,
and *Christ*, how it must've glowed.

Soon she'll all-the-way forget,
and we'll have to tell her
something different,
     something pieced together
     to fill in all this darkness,
     make our losses feel
     less permanent.

And some day she'll ask me,
and I'll know not what to say,
but until then,
I flick on the porch light
and let her relive
what I hope is so beautiful
it'll burn
our eyes blue.

Stardust to Stardust; or, Ancestry

Onion grass trimmings
and two-cycle exhaust fumes
smell like April
nights so clear
that space looks back down at us
like proud parents
at elementary school recitals.

Six-year-old Tim snaps
side-eyed over his shoulder,
    "Don't follow me you fucking moon."

He wants to do this on his own,
    and either way
        we'll all have to.

Weeding

I do not love
this tedious work,
plucking, one by one,
the small green sprouts from
their colonized homes
in the gardens hugging our house,
a one-man line-of-defense
against the choking out
of daisy, of bee balm, of tickseed,
and every other bright bit
of life we foster.

Still, finding myself
on quiet knees
beside the bed out front,
the one with the river birch
and some creeping phlox
my cousin planted,
I feel the slow drip
of calm in purpose,
and seeing all the sunlit hours
ahead, beds and beds of maple sprouts
popped for the picking,

I'll wrap myself in this work,
knowing how
my brain gets scared
when the chores are done,
everything tucked neatly in
the rearview, nothing
left to distract
me from myself.

On The Night My Pal Left Us I Was Working In The Yard

Sometimes it's hard to map
our paths, nothing
tied up neatly, all those roots
twisting below.

I was mulching, and simply
pushing life
into the ground
to quiet my own head,
little chores to keep
the blood flow.

It was spring.

There was no thought of grief
or the ways in which
our copings fail us,
and somewhere
in between the shoveling in,
the push of the barrow,
the turning and the steam,
he was gone.

I had no idea.

It was spring,
which I've already told you,
but it feels important to
keep mentioning.

This was not the time
to die.

Do you understand?

It was spring.

Say it with me:

    This is not the time to die.

Middle May

A dry
afternoon—
    not a lot of talk
    from the birds today.

After a Suicide

Sure,
things are mundane
mostly,
and terrible
as often as they're not.

I have no metaphor
about flowers, nothing
about the things that have
grown and died
to help it make sense.
Nothing to muffle
the ache.

And so the poet is useless,
a failure with so little
to offer you,

but here:

when you're knee deep
and it's just too much,
know that the voice in your head

is in mine too,
all the time talking
us straight toward the worst,
and so in this way
we're here together,
and so in this way
you're never alone.

Stay.

Please.

Poem for a Sick Child on the Fourth of July

Night again,
and the two of us rocking,
both wanting sleep,
while the neighboring farm blows off
the last of its mortars,
my hands still smelling of hose water
and Pink Brandywine leaves.

A small plastic giraffe
with big green eyes
and a pair of blue overalls
is digging
its outstretched arm into my hip
from its misplaced home
between the cushions of our glider.

Outside, as the celebration dims,
the night resigns itself again
to darkness, and your gut-sick body
finally slacks into mine.

        Yes,
you love me now

because, when your mother sleeps,
I am left of what you know,
    and yes,
in tomorrow's tired daylight
I will likely hide this toy giraffe
somewhere far from you and this chair
that has, tonight, assumed itself
our cradle.

For now, though, I will
breathe you in,
commit your tiny form to memory,
and stay here,
uncomfortable like this,
for as long as you will let me,
knowing how quickly
time takes us away
from who we've been.

Weepy On My Patio

In the soft darkness of an early Tuesday,
I listen
to the back-and-forth
of two owls
high above me.

Their voices echo through
the woods
like magic
    or an old friend—
       a hum heard only
          in the low rumbling
            of morning.

Eulogy

Despicable shit.
Enemy of joy.
Crawling each year
from the depths
of the furthest bed out back
to ransack my tomatoes,
feast on my bounty,
no thought of my months
of work, amended soil,
tracked sunlight,
or all the fostering of seedlings
popping in peat pots
on the bathroom sill.

Pea green asshole.
Purple horned cunt.
Insatiable super villain,
wreaking your havoc each year,
the last of which
did so while I traveled,
plants left vulnerable, unguarded,
destroying the Cherokees,
the Brandywines, and I

arriving home to nothing
but caged sticks and the fat culprit,
threw him to the creek
to be eaten by the green frogs, who,
even famished from mating,
ignored the thing,
maybe sharing in my contempt,
but probably knowing
its bellyful of nightshade.

And so there is no remorse
this time, finding it early
in its feast,
having followed its trail
of munched stems and balled turds
to where it hung
upside down,
plucking it from its meal,
muscles pulsing
in my gloved hand
(for I'll not bring myself to touch it bare)
and swiftly to the water with it,
where its writhing brought me somewhere
close to sympathy, but not
all the way, turning on my heels
to some other chore.

And yes, reading this now,
dangling as I am
on exaggeration
and anger misplaced,
you might try to think of this
as some attempt at metaphor,
something about our lofty goals
cut down,
or how everything we love will be
taken away if we're not
taken from it first.

But, friends, I am angry, and so here
is no attempt to enlighten,
no appeal to the greater good, at least
none of which I am aware.

Pull from it what you may,
but for now,
it's just me and the worm.

It's just me
and the worm.

Companion Planting

My daughter is learning
to recognize herself
in mirrors, squealing, *Me!*
bouncing red-blond curls,
hands clapping
in the joy of humid August
growth.

Today there are Nazis
burning torches in Virginia,
stretching our seams tight
like moth-chewed funeral suits
straining to cover
the sad growth
of our weak core.

I'm trying hard
to work on *Us,*
and to help her understand how,
in our garden out back,
that transcendence of
volunteers and heirloom grace,
the dill

and the basil
and the marigolds
work together like allied troops
    to keep the threats away
    so the yield may be stronger
        for its dependence on the other.

Self-Portrait

"To a worm in horseradish, the whole world is horseradish"
— Isaac Bashevis Singer

Pacing the backyard
scraping up
dog shit with a shovel
and hurling it
into the forest.

DNT PNIC

Sure, a few of the vowels are missing,
but I'm no dummy,
though rushing toward the next
inconsequential thing I have to do,
it takes a quarter mile or so to see
the out-of-state plate on this grey Ford Focus
that's going a little slow for my liking,
not clicking until the red light, when it hits me:

DNT PNIC

Like a message sent from somewhere
I've struggled lately
to find hope in,
        but I've struggled lately to find hope in most things,
        these last weeks again a spiraling
        mess of counting breaths,
        stomach full of worry
        over nothing I can name,
        and only minutes before this very moment,
        hollered into my windshield
                how long am I going to feel like this?

73

But glass is just polished sand,
and God's been tight-lipped lately,
so instead, I'll raise my *Amens* to you, generic dude
in your silver sedan, spreading the good word
of focus and calm at thirty miles per hour
across southeastern Pennsylvania,
slowing me down
right when I need to.

Three*

*the   ways   we   keep   ourselves   alive

Inward & Inward & Inward & Onward

None of these
transactions are easy.

None of these signs point
in any real direction.

How do we become
the people we'd love?

How do we
do better?

Curriculum

Today, before resuming
a lesson on the Buddhist perspective
of human nature,
my laptop calendar reminds me to
take a break from instruction
to recite a board-approved statement on school safety,
telling my students that, in the event of
an active shooter situation,
they can wear their backpacks backwards and hope
the books inside might shield their chest cavities
from the spray of bullets
coming, probably, from someone they sort of know,
who, probably, before finding himself here
with his father's unlocked "hunting rifle,"
had never broken a real law,
had never been in any real trouble,
had never given anyone cause to believe
he could wield a rage so overloaded,
and so now, with the sun
smashing through my classroom windows,
I explain that a thick textbook,
math maybe, or science,
can also be used to protect

the head and neck, and then
after the blood
finds its way back into our faces,
my shaky voice brings us back again
to Buddha, who teaches
that we all have in us this capacity
for love and violence,
and the class returns again
to their scribblings of hearts
and yinyangs,
eyes down,
never seeing
a thing.

Early Afternoon on the Gas-Hot Earth

Another sweat-stained Friday,
almost Halloween,
and a small girl is sitting on a concrete stoop
in a drooping Richard Nixon mask
scooping pumpkin flesh
out with bare hands
and slapping it
into a storm drain
dry with drought.

Someone is burning leaves nearby
and the air tastes
colder than it is.

The Man Across The Hall From My Grandmother Sleeps In His Funeral Suit

On top of the sheets, no less,
his final act of aggression, a *fuck off*
to the caretakers and the medicines
and the gravity working overtime
to hold him here.

Dressed to the nines, he lies
straight as an arrow,
stiff as a board,
coffin-composed,
door wide open for the world
to see, or maybe not
the world, but whatever he hopes comes next.

My grandma whispers,
the prettiest flowers get picked first

which explains her motives, too,
starved skeletal,
dentures gone,
nothing but that fluff of gray
poking from beneath

her blanketed bunker
under which, it seems, she plans to wait this out,
clinging so tight to what the other can't
give up,
praying for a Passover.

And so tonight, again,
after his daughter gives him the "pajama talk,"
and after I kiss my grandmother's paper-thin cheek
for what I'll later find out is the last time,
he'll shimmy out of his sweats,
don his black best,
make his bed, and hop on top
to wait for the darkness,
or the light,
or just anything
other than this.

Idols in Frames on Desks

Richard Brautigan is watching
from the corner,
staring through books,
glaring down like the swelling
    and breaking of some deep
    trout stream,
    while I write
    something about childhood
    or radishes
        over the howl
        of a deep, all-knowing wind.

Thanksgiving

Warm enough still
to turn the compost
without gloves on.

Middle of the Night Moon

Holy is the thing
on its slow dance across the night,
all chalk-faced and beaming,
filling the bedroom
with its ancient light, and peaking
through all the windows while I toss
over and over and over in the shine,
actually a little pissed
at how *not* dark tonight's dark is.

And normally I'd welcome
this bright peace,
having spent many a small hour pressed
against the window,
and just last month jostled my wife
awake, shirtless and giddy,
to watch the thing slip behind the earth
and vanish, singing
that Bonnie Tyler song as she burrowed
back beneath her pillows,
slinging groans and slanders
while the moon, too, tucked
itself into shadow.

But, no, this night is different,
up now for hours and begging
to return to the dream where, again,
my pal is singing songs
in some strange place,
    [this time a wood-paneled VFW hall
    that might also be my grandma's basement]
everyone drunk and bumping around
like moored boats in stormwater,
and at the end of his set
we're all wrecked
because he has to leave,
because of course he's dead,
and even our dream-selves understand,
blocking the door to keep him longer,
but just before he finally slips
out into the night,
and before I can slip out with him,
my sobbing shakes me
back into this bedroom, though unprepared
for the drenching light that's leaking
through the windows and all over,
making quick work
of brightening all the corners,
holding me alive here,
keeping me awake.

Vespers

When panic sits
on my chest in the night
and shows me things
that aren't there,
let me have breath
to breathe
and my wife
    to pull close
        like a life vest
            or a sheltering limb
        in a soaking
           summer rain.

Swimming 'Til Ya Can't See

Here's a soggy memory
of a basement bar in Brooklyn,
everything burned neon,
my shoes glued to the floor
by some other night's sick,
holler-talking
until the noise blurs
into one big sound
that's so loud I can
barely order another round
for me and my pal.
For here we've come to celebrate
a birth of sorts, a blossoming,
and so this is a night of hands on shoulders,
for balance, sure, but also for joy,
but as the whisky sinks in,
my eyes start doing that thing
where they don't quite see anymore
and I don't necessarily know
where my knees are, but
following his lead, the drinks

drop like shots, red faced and spinning,
and by now you have to know
how this ends.

Friends, I've spent
some nights at the drink,
it's true: these very words
should to you taste
thick, iodine and brine,
salt and sea-soaked as they are
in spirit.
I've been *that guy*,
ashamed to say,
painting the walls
in shit beer, filling sump pumps
with my furious insides, which is to say
I was not kind
to my adolescent self,
or my older self, either,
my twenty-sixth birthday finding me
deep in a bottle of absinthe,
a post-impressionist fairy hunter
so adrift in the wormwood
I believed I could read the bottle's
French label, channeling sixth grade
foreign language class, and yes,

I am telling you
I, one time, drank myself French,
    À votre santé
        and down
           I
               went.

But none of this training,
this organ-pickling,
this tempering of tolerance
proves useful now,
the walls doing that seasick swerve
and everyone soaked in cheer,
and while that isn't where this ends,
it's all I've held onto,
nothing else but guiding hands,
a taxi, and my friend, head over his shoulder,
hollering *text me, ya dick*
as he hovers away from me forever,
out into the New York night
I'll spend the rest of my life
begging to remember.

Reading Nietzsche In The Self-Help Section

That the wrens so quickly
made a home of the heavy gloves
left out by the woodpile all winter
should be proof enough
that our frantic scrapes for order
and blind attempts to name things
so to know them
are useless.

Fuck your essence, you
who predates the idea of *you*
and so will be a world
of people
and houses
as your hurdling changes course
with each fresh breath.

My Weatherworn American Flag of a Body

Think about it this way:

> Tiny bits of dried blood
> on my pale, chapped knuckles
> and the moon turns
> the snow in the backyard blue.

Vixen

for Rabbie Burns and our best-laid schemes

After pulling autumn's mums from their pots
and tucking the gardens in to sleep
beneath winter bedding of decorative hay,
I bring to the compost bin flint corn,
goose gourds,
and the too-small pumpkins
summer's over-raining stunted,
propping up the lid with a stick
and tossing it all, one by one, side-armed
over my shoulder into the heap.
And knowing my wife is likely watching
from the window,
I put a little *umph* into the final offering,
popping out my ass before dropping back
to a three-point fadeaway
so to make her laugh a bit
and forget, maybe for a minute even,
those loved we lost
to this year.

But coming to the pile now to turn,
billowing breath quickened by my folly
puffing out in December's drop,
I find what first I think is fuzz mold
sprouting from my laziness and absence from this work,
then recognize the red fluff of pelt,
and leaning further in, there she is—
caught dead, a fox,
her black muzzle wedged
through the pallet wood walls
of this unintentional trap, starved flat,
teeth white, nose wet, not from life,
but weather.

And with a backwards hop, pitchfork
up now like a weapon,
there is only the sound of my shuffling in the leaves
and modern prayers
[*Jesus Christ!* and *Holy Shit!* and the like]
to break the quiet of this place
to which I now am traitor.

Thinking not of the mice or chipmunks
or other small life now likely
praising me, their Artemis,
I free the thing, though far too late

to do real good,

and take her by the tiniest bit of tail, a lump

in my throat,

weaving around

downed limbs and rocks so not to bump her head

and add disrespect to my running list

of fresh offenses.

And coming to an acceptable place

near a bend in the creek,

far enough that my daughter

in her rain-booted splashing

will not see her breaking

back into the earth,

I leave her,

a whispered *I'm so sorry*

the only words I can summon for this service.

And all of this seems so foolish—

this poem for an animal I shouldn't care for,

did not know but for quick

glances and haunting shrieks in the night,

whose simple presence lived

as my wife's best case against the chickens

I've begged to bring here.

Foolish,

this simple grief at simple loss,

when our sorrow belongs already
to so much of the world.

But foolish as I am,
and trudging now away, eyes down
past the vacant mason bee house
and the bat box the bats won't use,
my head is a bucket of April plans
to mend this broken union
and turn our grief and pain back
to promis'd joy.

Four

{ *j* *o* *y* }

Melatonin Dreams & The Ending of Winter

I am remembering tonight
what happiness feels like—

    bare feet
    tracking black mulch across
    the hardwood foyer,

    the way little white flowers
    my wife calls *starlight*
    bloom sideways
    out of the quiet walls of the creek,
    swaying in the wind above
    shallow water
    crawling over swollen firewood
    tossed in, those drunken nights
    warmed then only by the closeness
    of our bodies,

    and my heart,
    slowly regaining itself,
    pacing with the cadence
    of the small green frogs,
    a call bouncing out of mud,

answered somewhere further off
in the early darkness
of morning.

Outside, Reading A Book On The Fourth Day Of Spring

Lazy as I am, and wanting not
to go inside and miss a second
of this ripe warmth,
I scoop the last lump of winter
into the dog's metal bowl
and return to my words,
quiet but for her lapping
and some over-joyous birds,
sun to my back, the dark outline of my head
eclipsing the page
behind which hovers
the evaporative ghosts of three months past,
rising up from the waterlogged lawn
and swirling around me
like the snuffed flames of winter pillars,
unhindered now,
licking the wind and dancing
in their freedom.

On An Afternoon In May A Bee Assumed My Wife A Flower

Imagine spotting her
from all the way across the yard,
what must've felt like miles
to the fuzzy little worker, who, seeing her
poking up from her patio chair
all wrapped in the ultraviolet wash
of daffodil and tulip,
made a beeline
straight past the dandelions
and the crocuses,
not slowing a bit
until reaching the target,
dancing just above her head,
at which point he must have known
she'd no pollen to offer,
but lingered awhile still,
hovering above
just basking,
feeling, probably, like he'd hit the jackpot,
like he'd died and gone
wherever bees hope they'll go,
and believe me, friend,

I get it,
and felt myself almost
say it out loud,
    I completely understand.

The Storm & Then The Daylight

This afternoon it opened up,
the wind and then
the rain and all that,
and the creek, thinking highly of itself,
left its depths and crawled
across the lawn so far
we thought it might just swallow
up our little plot, creeping
to our toes before turning back,
slurping into itself again
just in the nick,
right before the rot,
right before the ruin.

Do you see where I am going?

Last week the panic held
so tight that it just ached
and ached for days
on end, gulping
everything around,
all the muscles weak,
nothing left after.

Just now, though, I walked in sunlight,
barefoot to the mailbox,
dry pavement
warm on my toes,
not a cloud.

Sometimes the darkness
doesn't hold too long.

        Do you see where I am going?

Birds After Rain

Yes! And many!
Bursting chatter
from rain-soaked breasts
while we, too, poke
out from whatever storms
have kept us
hidden.

Dinner Prep

Using her thumbnail to slice
out the dark veins,
Leah says she's sorry
for the shrimp who die
with empty stomachs.

We all go wanting something, I say,
a shit joke that hardly lands.

But feeling the darkness
growing through the kitchen window,
we raise a toast
to the bubbling pot of bodies
swirling in their sea of salt
and the kale we cut
together
in the garden
just this morning.

June 1st

A humid morning—
    clapping my boots
    to shake out the spiders.

Curing

In two months' time
the garlic leaves will brown
and we will dig papery bulbs
from cedar darkness,
twisting them like widows' braids
to swing from the attic beam above
my dead grandfather's sawhorses.

In two months' time
my daughter will take wobbly steps,
an unripe tomato gripped tight
between her chubby fingers,
toward the June bug trap
we've warned her
away from again and again
with exaggerated eyebrows,
playfully stern.

In two months' time
I will look behind me,
shocked at my distance,
eyes to the creek rushing
storm water west,

and say something quiet,

mostly to myself,

about how fast it all goes,

or how I'm scared to go to sleep,

    each new dawn receding so quickly

        back to sunset.

To The Cat's Tail, Which Curves Like a River On The Carpet While She Sleeps

And all the other delicate
pleasures of life
quietly
at ease in this place—

the intermittent drip
in the sink
I'll not likely fix soon,

the gentle nesting noises
from the chickadees
moving in out back
[and oh, soon will come those tiny
chirpings, too],

the tapping of an untrimmed branch
at the window, which,
in a different type of poem
I suppose could suggest
a sort of fear,
but here, in the sunny spot
on the couch,

bare feet up and airing
on the sill,
there's nothing
but the smooth breaths,
the blood flow and the stillness.

July 4, 1995; or, The Monument Masons

Our backs
against mid-century headstones,
we watched explosions
of color
from a Polish cemetery
on a small, American, tree-lined Tuesday.

When the blasts bounced
back into nothing,
we ran
with sparklers, carving our names
in smoke
to drift and fade
with the others
    chasing echoes
    back up
    into darkness.

I Want To Call This Poem Hope

We'd thought last winter's flux
had finally drained the life from
our black locust,
its gaunt limbs growing
more brittle with each heavy snow.

But not having funds to rip it down,
the old, furrowed bastard stayed put,
and on nights with wind we slept
with forearms over foreheads
prepared for the crash.

But this spring,
and surprising even itself, I think,
that gnarled fucker pushed out
long helixed blooms
    and oh!
did the smell stone the bees
    and oh!
did we laugh and dance
in the snowfall of white petals—
       the joy of life not lost.

Sitting in its shade just now,
I'm thinking again of my friend
who went too early,
who thought, from the immediate look of it all,
he had no more color left
and fell out of this world.

Up through these branches, I'm looking
for some light
to dull the sting of this loss,
to scream into the world his hymn

    All is not lost, friends!

    All is not lost!

until my face is flushed with blood,
eyes wet from the spray of that far away
water I can't stop seeing
when I close them,
the unfathomable height dizzying me
so much that I've found myself
here on the ground,
steadying beneath this tree
that almost went down, too,
aware only now of a bird above me

singing for no one but the wind,
the blooms on my wife's honeysuckle vines
filling our air with summer,
and the pumping energy of life through
the roots beneath me,
a heartbeat rhythm so full of
our endless, changing futures.

Fuck this grief.

There's too much beauty here
for all of this grieving.

Some Days I Don't Need To Fake A Smile

Warm breezes in
the house, giddy
at the open windows.

I can sometimes live
on the other side
of this.

I can sometimes get
to where I want
to be.

Still Life At Dusk

Brilliant, right?
all of this, miraculous even,
the poetry of breath, of sweat,
of skin, so much that
some might holler *blasphemy!*
to the lot who don't spend every bit
of each day wandering in wonder
through the streets, taking each other
by the hands, giddy
at the blooming,
the color,
all the living.

And yeah, sure, I know
just as well as you that the whole of this
is often shit,
but come on, let's not hear that
now, for presently I am in the business
of making magic.
I want to fuck you up
on the world so you'll love it,
        so you'll stay.

And so here for you I'll do my best
to paint across
your mind like a canvas,
color-wash your field of vision,
make some beauty
where it shouldn't be,
or maybe where you just don't see it.

So let's start with the light,
that perfect light,
because of course the sun
is hanging low, exactly
as you're envisioning it,
everything all amber glow
just so, and setting
but never all the way,
no, not yet. A little longer,
please, as the bugs
work their way into our scene,
as there would be bugs
in this vision, wouldn't there,
making all their twitchy noises,
and birds, too, yes, of course,
tweets and clicks accordingly,
all that sweaty language
of nature dripping

into this new night
which I am building for us.
Go ahead, stick out your tongue.
Taste that humid air
thick with everything
hovering on it, the bees
sucking life into every clover flower
low enough for the mower blade to spare,
those back and forth lines
from the heft of it,
a little bit of order while the pumpkins
make some chaos with their vines, all wild
down the fence line.

Is this working?
Can you hear it?
The tinny music of an ice cream truck.
Maybe a little banjo?
Maybe some harp?
Maybe the sound of your mother's voice,
that song you'd fall asleep to
while she brushed back your hair
with her tired hands, her quiet voice,
    please don't take my sunshine away.

Yes, those fat gray clouds
are stuffed with rain, but no
they'll not drop it,
not here,
not on this day which we have
tucked ourselves into
together, to not let the hurt in,
to not let the life seep out.

What more could you want from the world?
All of your tunnels are bursting
with light.
All of the lenses are wide,
retinas gulping.

Sit in this beauty awhile.
There's still so much good
ahead.

The Second Coming

I'll make an end on it,
or so Ophelia said, wild
with grief, all lush with flowers,
and dropping into the water
that pulled her out of her own story.
But sentimental as I am,
and more afraid of endings
than I'll ever let on, I now play
this daily game of finding forwards,
hunting for new life
bristling beneath
each sunset,
every dropped curtain,
all this loss.

So look,
those bees again are rolling
their pollen-dusted bellies
across September's fade,
new life in their swirling even now,
at what should be an end
but instead will be mouthfuls
of carrots and greens

and giant sunflowers heading
straight into autumn's darkness.

Or there,
the maple whirligigging its rotors
all over my existence;
a pain in the ass, sure,
but with each new shoot a shout
to carry on,
to keep going.

Or here,
this tomato plant
climbing out of its cage, toppling the peppers,
and hopping the fence,
is the great, great, great, great grandchild
of my grandad's crop,
which, wanting not to disappear with him,
hitchhiked in some bird shit
from his tilled-under garden
to his front yard,
stretched up like a flagpole,
and grew tall to spite his absence
before turning over its seeds,
coming back each year now
to stand at the head of my raised bed,

weighed down by fruit that tastes
so much like my childhood
I should cry, but instead
let us rejoice!
Because there is life happening everywhere!
And all of this living is cause for celebration!

This waking,
this forward marching,
this banging together of limbs,
this clatter of existence,
and so all will be new again,
and so you, too, will be new again,
and so let us revel,
so let us love,
so let us have some color,
some mirth,
some fireworks,
or lightning,
which I learned last week
does the work of fertilization,
turning atmospheric nitrogen my garden can't lasso
into a tool it'll use to blossom, to burst
into new life, and forgive me
if my red-faced hysterics,
my belly laughing and clumsy frolicking

are off-putting in these times
when all around us is collapse,

but just last night,
as the rain rolled out to some other conquest,
thunder bouncing off itself
like drunks in the night,
my wife called me into the room,
wide eyed and beautiful,
and friends,
there is no way to talk about
the piss stick drying
into double lines on the sill
without, of course, the heat
and its blips of backlit
trees through the window—

Flashes of light.

Flashes of life.

Flashes of joy.

If you feel that you or someone you know is at immediate risk of death or serious harm please urgently call 999 (UK) or 800-273-8255 (US) to speak to someone who can help.

Notes

Some of these poems were first loosed upon the world through a handful of lovely magazines near and far.

Thanks to:

Barren Magazine: *Vixen*

Bitterzoet Magazine: *July 4th, 1995; or, The Monument Masons* and *Bloom* (originally published as *A Blossom In Spring*)

Frogpond Haiku: *June 1st* (originally published as *July 27th*)

The Hoot Review: *All Of What We Pass Along & All We Keep Inside*

Hypertrophic Literary: *Curing, Melatonin Dreams & The Ending Of Winer, Poem For A Sick Child On the Fourth Of July, Out Past The Light Of The Moon,* and *Sartre In My Nursery*

The Moth: *Stardust To Stardust; or, Ancestry*

Pidgeonholes Magazine: *I Want To Call This Poem Hope* and *Lungs*

Short Édition: *Middle Of The Night Moon* and *DNT PNIC*

Toho Journal: *The Man Across The Hall From My Grandmother Sleeps In His Funeral Suit* (nominated for the Pushcart Prize)

A recorded version of *I Want To Call This Poem Hope* with music by Jeff Zeigler was released alongside Laurie Cameron's *Honest Man* as part of the *All Is Not Lost* vinyl collaboration to benefit the Tiny Changes charity organization.

Out Past The Light Of The Moon was originally written to celebrate the joyous marriage of Megan and Joe Balaguer. Cheers to them!

The epigraph at the beginning of the collection was taken from: *Spring* by Ali Smith (Anchor Books).

The epigraph in *Self Portrait* was taken from a TED talk given by Malcolm Gladwell and can be attributed to Isaac Bashevis Singer.

The bones used in the making of the cover were ethically sourced.

Acknowledgements

Let's first deliver the biggest bundle of thanks to my wife, Leah, who protects me from myself and helps me love this life in a way I otherwise could not. There's not a strong enough way to explain her kindness or the love I have for her.

Thanks to my family for their depthless well of support. A bunch of balloons, all which read "THANKS" to Rich Appel, great friend and poet extraordinaire, for editing these poems with fresh eyes and a generous heart. None of my poems would be what they are without him. Thanks so, so much to Maggie Smith for joining me on this joyous journey. A freshly dried and pressed bouquet of thanks to Helen Ahpornsiri for the beautiful artwork. Thanks to the friends who read this collection in its awkward stages, who pushed me to keep writing, who held me up, especially Daniel DiFranco, Nick Gregorio, Kirk Johnson, and John McGraw. Thanks, too, to Kelli Russell Agodon, Sean Carey, "Fun" Fran Levitt-Higgins, and Frank Turner for all of their kindness. A suitcase full of thanks to Brian Hexter for organizing the Joy tour and getting this book out into the wild. Thanks to Summer and the Unsolicited Press team for crawling back into the weeds with me. Thanks to the Tiny Changes team for upholding and honoring Scott Hutchison's legacy.

And thanks to you, reader. You mean the world to me, and I hope you found some joy here.

About the author

Francis Daulerio is a poet and teacher from Blue Bell, Pennsylvania. He received his MFA in Creative Writing from Arcadia University in 2014 before releasing *If & When We Wake* (Unsolicited Press 2015) and *Please Plant This Book* (The Head & The Hand Press 2018), both with illustrations by Scottish artist, Scott Hutchison. Francis has also released *All Is Not Lost,* a collaborative vinyl EP of poetry-infused music to benefit the Tiny Changes charity organization, and *With a Difference* (Trident Boulder 2020), a split book of 'covers' with Philadelphia author Nick Gregorio.

Francis is a mental health awareness advocate and has performed in the United States and abroad to raise money for suicide prevention. He lives in the woods with his wife and children. He finds a good bit of joy there.

More information can be found at www.FrancisDaulerio.com

About the Press

Unsolicited Press is a small publishing house in Portland, Oregon and is dedicated to producing works of fiction, poetry, and nonfiction from a range of voices, but especially the underserved. The team is comprised of hardworking volunteers that are passionate about literature.

Learn more at www.unsolicitedpress.com.

Find the team on Twitter and Instagram: @unsolicitedp

A portion of the proceeds from this collection will go to Tiny Changes, a nonprofit dedicated to supporting mental health and suicide prevention.

Learn more about Tiny Changes at tinychanges.com

CPSIA information can be obtained
at www.ICGtesting.com
Printed in the USA
LVHW111404210622
721790LV00006B/497